In memory of
Richard Jackson,
editor and friend

𝒜
atheneum

ATHENEUM BOOKS FOR YOUNG READERS • An imprint of Simon & Schuster Children's Publishing Division • 1230 Avenue of the Americas, New York, New York 10020 • © 2021 by Brian Floca • Book design © 2021 by Simon & Schuster, Inc. • UNITED STATES POSTAL SERVICE®, USPS Corporate Signature, USPS Letter Carrier Uniform and USPS Long Life Vehicle (LLV) are trademarks of the United States Postal Service and are used with permission. • New York City Police and Fire Department logos, the Department of Sanitation New York, and TLC used with permission of the City of New York. • All rights reserved, including the right of reproduction in whole or in part in any form. • ATHENEUM BOOKS FOR YOUNG READERS is a registered trademark of Simon & Schuster, Inc. Atheneum logo is a trademark of Simon & Schuster, Inc. • For information about special discounts for bulk purchases, please contact Simon & Schuster Special Sales at 1-866-506-1949 or business@simonandschuster.com. • The Simon & Schuster Speakers Bureau can bring authors to your live event. For more information or to book an event, contact the Simon & Schuster Speakers Bureau at 1-866-248-3049 or visit our website at www.simonspeakers.com. • The text for this book was set in Helvetica Neue LT. • The illustrations for this book were rendered in watercolor, ink, acryclic, and gouache. • Manufactured in China • 0221 SCP • First Edition • 10 9 8 7 6 5 4 3 2 1 • Library of Congress Cataloging-in-Publication Data • Names: Floca, Brian, author, illustrator. • Title: Keeping the city going / Brian Floca. • Description: First edition. | New York : Atheneum Books for Young Readers, [2021] | "A Caitlyn Dlouhy Book." | Audience: Ages 4–8. | Audience: Grades K–1. | Summary: "An ode to the essential workers keeping the country operating during the COVID-19 pandemic"—Provided by publisher. Includes author's note. • Identifiers: LCCN 2020036623 | ISBN 9781534493773 (hardcover) | ISBN 9781534493780 (ebook) • Subjects: CYAC: Community workers—Fiction. | City and town life—Fiction. | Quarantine—Fiction. | COVID-19 (Disease)—Fiction. • Classification: LCC PZ7.F6579 Kee 2021 | DDC [E]—dc23 • LC record available at https://lccn.loc.gov/2020036623

KEEPING
THE CITY
GOING

BRIAN FLOCA

A Caitlyn Dlouhy Book

Atheneum Books for Young Readers

atheneum NEW YORK LONDON TORONTO SYDNEY NEW DELHI

We are here at home now,
watching the world though our windows,
and wondering what will happen next.

Outside, we see the city we know,
but not as we've seen it before.

Outside, the city is strangely still.
Store doors are locked
and their windows are dark
and our neighbors all stay hidden.
The voice of the city is low,
and the streets are almost empty.

Almost, but not entirely.

There are still some people out on the streets,
driving this and that, heading from here to there.
They might be family, friends, or strangers.
They're there because we need them.

They're the people keeping the city going.

They're the people out delivering food—
sometimes to us, and right to our doors;
a breakfast, a lunch, or a dinner . . .

And sometimes to stores,
and more than one meal—
enough to fill the empty shelves.

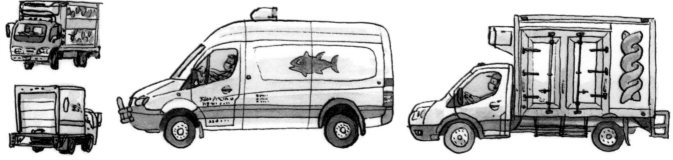

SPICES
BEANS
FLOURS
OILS

DRY
FRUITS
& NUTS

They're the people on the buses and trains,
those who keep them moving,
and those who ride them, too . . .

who are heading out to keep grocery stores open,
to sell to the city
beans and flour and rice
and soap and soup and spaghetti . . .

They're the people keeping the city clean.

(You know, pretty clean.)

They're delivering letters and packages—
boxes full of things people need
but can't go out to buy.

And maybe . . .

just maybe, they're bringing
that *one* thing we ordered
that we don't really need . . .

but we've been stuck here at home,
and we're *bored*, and we bought it.

(We'll try not to do it again.)

They're out on the street (and under the street)
keeping water, gas, and electricity flowing.

They're keeping the phones and the internet working,
helping us feel not so alone, helping us stay connected
with streaming shows and video calls,
and our teachers and classes and story times, too.

They're the people in charge of putting out fires . . .

and the people whose job is to keep everyone safe.

They're the paramedics and the EMTs,
taking people to the care that they need.

They're the doctors and nurses,
the technicians and aides and clerks and cleaners,
everyone working through long days and worry
to help patients heal.

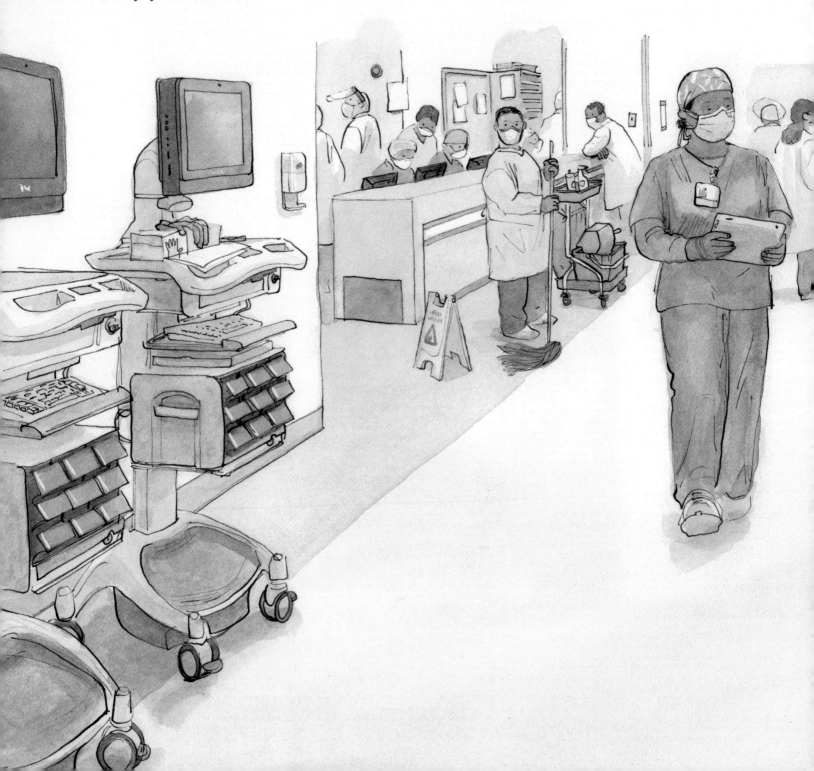

We see the city, strangely still,
and we miss our friends and neighbors,
and we miss the voice of the city.

But we see the people still out on the streets,
and whether they're family, friends, or strangers,
we see the work they're doing.

And every evening, at seven o'clock . . .

we open our windows
and lean out and look,
and lean out and listen.

We see the city we know,
but not as we've seen it before.

We see our neighbors again,
now at their windows
and now on stoops,
on balconies, and roofs.

And we hear the voice of the city,
but not as we've heard it before:
the sounds at first are low—
a clap, a whistle, a call.

The sounds are low, and then they grow—
pots BANG! Drums BOOM!
Bells RING! Horns BLOW!—
a racket, a din, and a row!

We join with our clapping,
we join with a CHEER!

We hear the city say to us—
and we say back to the city—
that we are all still here,
and we are here together.

We hear the city say,
and we say with the city—
and we all say together—
thanks to the people
still out on the streets,
driving this and that,
going from here to there,
and taking care of the sick.

**Thanks to the people
keeping our city going.**

Author's Note

I have enjoyed sketching the places and people of New York City since I first moved here, over twenty years ago now. In the spring of 2020, with the arrival of COVID-19, drawing what I saw around me in the city took on an additional meaning and purpose; it became one small way of trying to stay oriented in a place that felt suddenly transformed and unfamiliar, locked down and hushed, an Edward Hopper canvas come to life.

I found myself pulled, in particular, to the vehicles still out on the streets, the stubborn exceptions to the city's new stillness. (We all have our coping mechanisms, and drawing vehicles is apparently one of mine.) Operating those trucks, ambulances, and more were the people who perform the essential work that has always been required to get New York from one day to the next: the people who stock the stores, who keep the city safe and fed and clean and running, and who take care of the sick. In a city as large and busy as New York, their work is notable on the most regular of days. In the midst of a pandemic, the steady carrying-on of that work became remarkable.

As the drawings began to accumulate, I began writing, wondering if there might be a way to organize the material into something that could speak to young people about these strange and challenging days. I took additional inspiration from neighbors I could hear cheering every evening at seven o'clock, through the spring. Home from school and home from work, isolated and with stresses and struggles of their own, they were sounding from their windows and stoops a daily expression of gratitude toward healthcare and other workers still on the job—cheers we cannot imagine to be all we owe those workers, but that helped lift morale in the early, overwhelming days of the pandemic, when the lift was badly needed.

It feels both meaningful and fraught to make a book about this difficult moment, about a crisis that, at this writing, continues to touch so many people, so deeply, and in so many different ways. I didn't intend to and certainly don't imagine I have made a book covering every aspect of these events, but I'm grateful to Caitlyn Dlouhy and Michael McCartney and everyone at Atheneum for the chance to make a book about a part of them. An Italian physician was quoted in the *New York Times Magazine* in April: "Since the beginning, I have thought of the words of John Paul II: It is necessary that the heroic becomes daily and that the daily becomes heroic." That was the city I saw out my window and on walks this spring, and it is a glimpse of that city that I hope readers will find in this book.

—B. F.
Brooklyn, New York, November 2020